Beep, beep, goes Sheep

Sheep looks as Farmer Walt parks the jeep.

Sheep spots the keys and the wallet. Goat and Cow nod and wink.

Beep! Beep! Sheep, Goat and Cow zip past the shed. They zoom past the swamp.

They want to get to town very quickly.

"What a treat," grins Cow.
Goat has her hair washed.
Cow has her fringe curled.

Sheep's wool is clipped.
Watch it turn pink!

Cow gets high-heeled boots. Goat and Sheep get fancy coats. Watch as they wander down the street and grin.

"I want to try that cap," says Goat. She swaps the hat with swan feathers for Cow's red cap.

"We want them all," laughs Sheep. She pulls the cash from the wallet.

Goat takes a long sip of milkshake and swallows. "What a treat!" grins Sheep. "I want extra milk," grins Cow.

"What a fun day," says Goat.
"That was the best," says Cow.

They zoom past the swamp and back past the shed.

Sheep sits to watch as Farmer Walt wanders to the jeep. "What is this?" says Farmer Walt.

Goat bleats and Cow moos.
Sheep winks at them.

Words to blend

wallet	swamp	want
what	washed	Walt
wander	swaps	swan
swallows	was	bleats
farmer	quickly	feathers
zoom	extra	high-heeled

Beep, beep, goes Sheep   Level 7, Set 2a, Story 100

Before reading

Synopsis: Sheep drives Goat and Cow into town for a fun day of hairdressing and shopping using Farmer Walt's jeep and wallet.

Review phonemes and graphemes: /ear/ ere, eer; /air/ are, ear, ere; /j/ ge, dge, g; /s/ c, ce, sc, se, st; /c/ ch; /u/ o, o-e, ou; /e/ ea; /r/ wr; /ar/ a, al

Focus phoneme: /o/   **Focus grapheme:** (w)a

Story discussion: Look at the cover, and read the title together. Ask: *What is happening in the picture? What do you think might happen next?* Allow children to share ideas, then ask: *Do you think this book will be fiction or non-fiction? How do you know?*

Link to prior learning: Remind children that the sound /o/ as in 'top' can also be spelled 'a', and that this usually only happens after W or Qu. Turn to page 10 and ask children to point out the words where 'a' makes an /a/ sound, and the words where 'a' makes an /o/ sound.

Vocabulary check: wander: another way of saying 'walk slowly'.

Decoding practice: Display the words 'wallet', 'swamp', 'what' and 'washed'. Can children read each word, and circle the part that makes the /o/ sound?

Tricky word practice: Display the word 'watch'. Remind children that the tricky part of this word is 'tch', which says /ch/. How quickly can children find and read this word in the book? Tell children that 'a' in this word makes the focus sound for the book /o/.

After reading

Apply learning: Discuss the book. Ask: *Do you think the things Sheep and friends did looked like fun? Do you think Farmer Walt would be happy if he found out? Why do you think this?*

Comprehension

- Who got their hair washed? (Goat)
- Who got high-heeled boots? (Cow)
- Do you think Farmer Walt knows what happened? Why or why not? (any reasoned answer)

Fluency

- Pick a page that most of the group read quite easily. Ask them to reread it with pace and expression. Model how to do this if necessary.
- In pairs, children can read pages 10–11, taking turns to read a sentence aloud. Encourage them to read clearly and steadily, and to read Goat and Sheep's words so it sounds like they are really talking.
- Practise reading the words on page 17.

Tricky words review

watch	to	says
many	again	laughs
once	because	said
have	our	one
thought	through	two